To Phil.
Happy fortieth
October 1994

Best wishes
Janette & Richard

**Raymonds Photographers & Press Agency**

# Images of

# Derby County

# Raymonds Photographers & Press Agency

## Images of
# Derby County

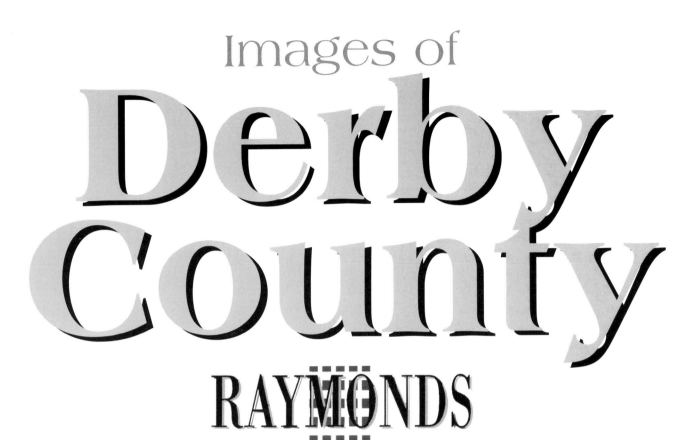

RAYMONDS
PRESS AGENCY
news • sport • pictures

Photographers
*Raymonds*

A N T O N   R I P P O N

Breedon Books
Publishing Company
Derby

First published in Great Britain by
The Breedon Books Publishing Company Limited
44 Friar Gate, Derby, DE1 1DA.
1995

**Dedication**

This book is dedicated to the Derby County players portrayed in this book, and to the Raymonds photographers who braved all weathers to record their deeds.

**Acknowledgements**

The author wishes to thank Les Parkin of Raymonds Photographers, who readily agreed to this project and gave it his full support; and Nicholas Jacoby, also of Raymonds, who was unstinting in his help and advice when it came to viewing the many thousands of images from which those that make up this book were selected.

Special thanks must go to Breedon Books' Pip Southall, who researched each image and produced much of the information from which the captions were written.

ISBN 1 85983 025 0

Printed and bound by Butler & Tanner, Somerset.
Cover printed by Premier Print, Nottingham.

# Foreword

by Les Parkin
Managing Director, Raymonds Photographers

CAMERAMEN from Raymonds Press Agency have been photographing Derby County's matches at the Baseball Ground for more than 40 years. During that time they have taken many thousands of photographs which have captured memorable and historic moments in the club's recent history and the pictures have appeared in newspapers, magazines and on television all over the world.

Now we are delighted to have been given the opportunity by Rams historian Anton Rippon and Breedon Books to open our files and share the contents with supporters.

Few of us realise at the time that we are witnessing historic moments. But trawling through our negatives gave us a constant reminder that we had done just that – and it became an enthralling exercise.

From the down years in the Fifties, when after winning the FA Cup at Wembley in 1946, the Rams dropped into ignominy in the Third Division North, through the rise up two divisions to the glory years of being League champions and playing in Europe, to the Nineties and the current battle to get back to the big time, Raymonds cameramen have been recording history.

For us, of course, it has been just part of doing our job which can sometimes be infuriating and frustrating, but never dull. The camera never lies, but what is remarkable is the way that football pictures have changed over the years.

In the early days before automatic cameras and telephoto lenses and high-speed films, photographers lay on groundsheets behind the goal using cumbersome plate cameras and trying to avoid players careering into them in the heat of the match.

As the game unfolded they had to press the button at precisely the right time to capture an action shot and there were no second chances as there are with today's fast-moving equipment.

Modern photographs are technically superb with excellent close-up detail. But in 50 years time people looking at them will never guess where they were taken – it could be on any ground in the country.

There is no doubt, however, where the photographs in this book were taken – the atmospheric drama of the Baseball Ground is there even though many changes have taken place.

We have been privileged to be a witness to some of the Rams' magic moments and are delighted that Breedon Books has given us the opportunity to allow fans to relive a few of them through our photographic archives.

# Introduction

I SAW my first Derby County match in 1952. It was just before Christmas and Stoke City were the visitors to the Baseball Ground. It was memorable because the Rams won 4-0, with Jack Stamps and Jack Lee both amongst the scorers. Such success fired my enthusiasm and I became a fan. A couple of weeks later they were at home again. It was my birthday and again they scored four goals and won, this time against Bolton Wanderers, Nat Lofthouse and all. On Boxing Day, Sunderland had three put past them at the Baseball Ground and by now I was on a high. Following this team was just too good to be true. They won every week …and there were plenty of goals, too.

Of course, it didn't last. In fact, it didn't last to the extent that at the end of the season Derby County were relegated, rock bottom of the old First Division, although even then they beat Manchester City 5-0 with three games to go. Things went from bad to worse, however. The following season Derby struggled in the Second Division and in 1955 they finished bottom again to tumble into the Third Division North, for the first time in the club's history. As one supporter put it some time later, 'it was from caviar to fish and chips'.

I've never found anything much wrong with fish and chips, though, and those two seasons of Third Division football remain the

On 20 September 1969, Raymonds photographers were at the Baseball Ground to capture scenes which can now never be repeated. The Rams were back in the top flight, Brian Clough had set the town alight and when Tottenham Hotspur visited Derby a record crowd of 41,826 jammed themselves into the ground and saw the Londoners hammered 5-0. Here, fans at the Osmaston End celebrate a goal.

highlight of my football-watching days. In the first of those seasons the Rams finished runners-up to Grimsby Town and, as only one team was promoted in those pre-Play-off days, Derby stayed where they were. A year later they were on the way back, crowned Northern Section champions after two seasons in which they scored 222 goals and enjoyed battles with the likes of Accrington Stanley, Hartlepools United, Workington and Barrow.

I had three particular heroes from that team, Tommy Powell, Reg Ryan and Geoff Barrowcliffe, and many years later they became my friends. I'm now of an age where I fail to be impressed by contemporary sporting heroes, but the sight of Tommy Powell hurrying down Derby's Victoria Street, that slightly hunched, stooping gait carrying him through a crowd of shoppers just like he used to weave his way down Derby's wing, still pleases me.

Everyone, of course, has their heroes. A supporter who was perhaps 14 when Derby County won their first League championship under Brian Clough in 1972, will no doubt get a similar tingle today when he glimpses Kevin Hector or John O'Hare in one of Derby's crowded streets. My doctor, several years younger than me, moved to a new surgery and asked if I could obtain for him two large photographs to decorate the wall of the waiting room. I assumed it was bygone Derby that he wished to illustrate but, no, he said it was Derby County. And could it please be Alan Hinton or someone from that era? We all have our heroes. And photographs are a way in which we can always have our heroes with us.

When I began watching the Rams, Raymonds Photographers were also starting to record their matches and for the last 40 years or so their images have appeared in a wide variety of national magazines and

In the early 1970s, Rams manager Brian Clough was in constant demand for public appearances. Here, Raymonds were on hand when the great man obliged shoppers turned autograph hunters at a local grocery store.

Over 20 years later and Brian Clough is back at the Baseball Ground, sitting next to Rams owner Lionel Pickering. In the years after his controversial departure Clough's shadow had haunted successive Derby managers and he was never far from supporters' thoughts, most of whom dreamed that he would one day return as manager again. It was never to be and in March 1995, now a shadow of his former self, he came back to present a long-service award. Of course, he received a tumultuous reception.

newspapers. In the early days, as Les Parkin writes, the photographer had only one chance to capture an incident, but somehow he seldom missed it; today, motor-driven cameras afford a much better chance. Some 40 years ago the prints were produced from large glass-plate negatives; today, 35mm full colour is the name of the game. Requirements have changed, too. Where once goalmouth action was imperative, today many clients require close-ups of boots and logo-laden shirts, perhaps for an advertising feature. But whatever the changes in technology or requirements, sheer professionalism on the part of the photographer is essential. And down these four decades, Raymonds men have certainly possessed that.

It is particularly appropriate that so many of the images in this book show the old Popular Side of the Baseball Ground, both with the Toyota Stand (or Ley Stand or Co-op Stand to give it its previous names) towering over it and in its days before 1969, when the Pop Side was simply roofed and advertised Offilers Ales to the angels. At the time of writing the area is to become all-seater to end an era which has lasted since the ground became Derby County's permanent home 100 years ago.

But whether your memories, your heroes, belong to those days when the height of sophistication was a short-back-and-sides and a pair of Stanley Matthews CWS football boots, or the Swinging Seventies of long hair

The fans didn't know it – although most probably guessed it – but when Roy McFarland said goodbye to the Pop Side in April 1995, he was also saying goodbye to Derby County itself after 28 years as player, coach and manager, interrupted only by a brief spell at Bradford City. Here McFarland acknowledges the fans in the main stand, his face telling the story. His brief was promotion. He failed, albeit in very difficult circumstances as he had to rebuild the team and cut the wage bill. Flanking him are (from left to right) Jason Kavanagh, Paul Williams and on-loan goalkeeper Russell Hoult from Leicester City. The result of the game is best forgotten.

and skimpy shorts, or when the trend towards multi-coloured goalkeeper's jerseys and ubiquitous 'away strips' had taken hold, this book will have something for you. Whether your hero be Ray Straw, Kevin Hector, Bobby Davison or Dean Saunders – or anyone of the hundreds of footballers who have worn a Derby County shirt since the early Fifties – you'll probably find him here. And I hope it gives you a tingle, too.

Anton Rippon
Derby
May 1995

# The Fifties

Some Rams fans were still thinking wistfully of Carter, Doherty, Stamps and company. For others it was a time memorable for two high-scoring seasons of Third Division football.

Former Derby County and England centre-half Jack Barker, pictured here when he took over as manager at the Baseball Ground in November 1953, had the unenviable task of averting a crisis. But, fine player though Barker was, he lacked the managerial skills required to stop a once-great club from plunging still further into the depths.

Derby County's staff before the start of the 1954-55 season, pictured in the Baseball Ground gymnasium. These were dark days for the Rams, who were on the verge of completing a drop from the First Division to the Third Division North within three seasons. Post-war stars like Reg Harrison (fourth from left, front row), who had gained an FA Cup winners' medal in 1946, and Bert Mozley (sixth from left, second row), a former England full-back, were each in their last season with the Rams. It was left to men like Jack Parry and Geoff Barrowcliffe (first and second from left, back row) and Tommy Powell (third from left, second row) to help Derby back from the lower reaches of the Football League.

In July 1955, with the club facing Third Division football for the first time, the Rams board turned to another former Derby and England player when they asked Harry Storer, pictured here (right) with Derby County chairman Oswald Jackson, to take over as manager.

Harry Storer at his desk at the Baseball Ground on the day he took over as manager of Derby County. Storer came from a local sporting family. His father, also Harry, kept goal for Liverpool and Woolwich Arsenal and played cricket for Derbyshire, while his uncle William played for the Rams and kept wicket for Derbyshire and England. Storer brought with him the reputation of a fearsome manager who had done well in charge of Coventry City and Birmingham City.

One of Harry Storer's first jobs was to find an inspirational captain to take his ideas on to the field. He knew the man he wanted: West Bromwich Albion's Irish international wing-half or inside-forward Reg Ryan, who had helped Albion win the FA Cup the previous year. Here, Storer introduces Ryan to another fearsome character, the manager's dog Billy. Perhaps Billy's reputation was undeserved though; the black cat in the background certainly seems unconcerned.

Derby County's first-ever match in the Third Division North was, unusually for a Saturday, an evening match against Mansfield Town on 20 August 1955. South African Alf Ackerman (two), Albert Mays and Jesse Pye, a former Wolves and England forward, helped the Rams to a 4-0 win. In this picture Jack Parry (far right) watches the ball flash across the face of the Stags' goal. Other Derby players in the picture are Tommy Powell (in the distance) and Ken Harrison.

A happy crowd in the 'Boy's Pen' at the Baseball Ground before the Third Division North game against Workington in October 1955, the Cumbrian club's first-ever League meeting with the Rams. Many of the boys are still wearing school uniform – no designer leisure wear in those days – and they are all being rallied by the Rams mascot, dressed in black and white, sporting a top hat and ringing a handbell. The Boy's Pen was situated at the Normanton End of the ground adjacent to a small section for disabled supporters. In the mid-1950s it cost 9d (about 4p) for a schoolchild to watch Derby County from that special and always over-subscribed enclosure.

Now only Associate Members of the Football League following their relegation from Division Two, the Rams were obliged to take part in the first round proper of the FA Cup and in November 1955 they were held to a 2-2 draw at Northern League side Crook Town. In the Wednesday afternoon replay, however, Derby ran out easy 5-1 winners with Ray Straw getting a hat-trick. Here Straw (far right) lashes in a shot at the Crook goal. Alas, in the next round another non-League side, Boston United, hammered the Rams 6-1 at the Baseball Ground. It was one of the Cup sensations of all time, made all the more amazing by the fact that Boston include no less than six former Derby players.

In their first season in the Third Division North the Rams were beaten to the only promotion place by Grimsby Town, who were led by the former Manchester United centre-half Allenby Chilton. The following year, though, the Rams won the title outright, scoring 111 League goals, one more than the previous season. In September 1956, the Rams hammered Halifax Town 6-0. This picture shows some rare action around the Derby goal where 'keeper Terry Webster watches a shot go narrowly wide. The Derby defenders pictured from left to right are Roy Martin, Martin McDonnell and Reg Ryan.

In 1956-57 former Ilkeston miner Ray Straw equalled the Rams' record for League goals by one player in a single season with 37, the same number that Jack Bowers scored in 1930-31 from 11 fewer games than Straw. Here, Straw is beaten to the ball by Carlisle United goalkeeper Tom Fairley and although the Rams won 3-0, the centre-forward failed to score on this occasion.

In December 1956, Derby County were again the victims of an FA Cup shock, this time when Lancashire Combination side New Brighton, who had lost their Football League place in 1951, won 3-1 in the second round at the Baseball Ground before a crowd of over 23,000. Terry Webster prepares to block a shot from the non-Leaguers as Roy Martin and Martin McDonnell move in.

Back in the Second Division, the Rams made a bad start to the 1957-58 season, losing their first three matches including this one, the first home game of the season when Barnsley won 4-1. Ray Young (on the line) and goalkeeper Terry Webster look deflated as Barnsley score again. The other Rams players are Martin McDonnell and Glyn Davies.

At the end of the 1957-58 season Harry Storer signed two experienced forwards in Johnny Hannigan (left) and Dave Cargill (right). Hannigan cost £6,000 from Sunderland, where he had been one of the players involved in an illegal bonuses scandal in the days of maximum wages for footballers. He could play either on the wing or at centre-forward and did well for the Rams before moving to Bradford. Cargill, a left winger who cost £4,250, had a reasonable first season but began to suffer weight problems and was eventually sold to Lincoln City.

Jack Parry puts Derby 1-0 ahead against First Division Preston North End at the Baseball Ground in January 1959. The Rams looked like springing an FA Cup shock over Preston, then one of the leading clubs in the country, until Albert Mays played a back-pass which stuck in the snow and allowed Preston to equalise. The game ended 2-2 and Derby lost the replay 5-2 at Deepdale, Dave Cargill scoring both their goals, one from the penalty spot.

In 1958-59 Derby County put together a ten-match unbeaten run and eventually ended the season in seventh place in Division Two. Included in that run was this 3-1 win over Scunthorpe United on a snow-covered Baseball Ground pitch in mid-January. Rams goalkeeper Ken Oxford tips the ball over the bar watched by Rams players (from left to right) Roy Martin, Glyn Davies, George Darwin, Les Moore and Albert Mays.

# The Sixties

For Derby County the Sixties began to swing only when they were nearly over. But from Storer via Ward to Clough, each manager brought some fine players to the Baseball Ground.

A scramble in the mud for Derby's Barry Hutchinson against struggling Leeds United at the Baseball Ground on Christmas Eve 1960. Gerry Francis is the nearest Leeds defender and the other is Freddie Goodwin. The Rams lost 3-2, both their goals coming from Derbyshire opening batsman Ian Hall (right).

Jack Parry (nearest camera) and Glyn Davies watch as the ball scrapes agonisingly past the Manchester United post at the Baseball Ground in January 1960 when over 33,000 spectators saw United win a third-round FA Cup-tie 4-2. The United goalkeeper is Harry Gregg, the players back helping in defence are Dennis Viollet and (partly hidden) Bill Foulkes, Derby's Peter Thompson and United's Albert Quixall are to the right of the picture. Six years later United won 5-2 in another third-round tie at Derby.

April 1961 and veteran forward Tommy Powell shakes hands with Frank Upton before the home game against Ipswich Town. Powell had announced his retirement and this was due to be his final appearance but he was ruled out by injury. He made a brief comeback the following season before, ironically, a crude tackle from a Portsmouth defender in a League Cup match finally ended his career. Also in the line-up (from left to right) are Ray Swallow, Peter Thompson, Bill Curry, Ray Young and Tony Conwell. Geoff Barrowcliffe, Powell's greatest pal at the Baseball Ground, is hidden behind Upton.

As he examines a Football League long-service statuette, Tommy Powell, veteran of 406 League and Cup appearances for Derby County, perhaps reflects on his long Rams career which began as a 16-year-old grammar schoolboy during World War Two.

Cheers! Former Rams players toast mine host of Belper's Talbot Inn. The landlord, Jack Robson (right) played for Derby County from 1928 to 1932. Three former England forwards are at the front of the bar: Harry Bedford (extreme left), George Thornewell (second from the right) and Sammy Crooks (extreme right). How much would such a trio command in today's inflated transfer market?

Former Coventry, Chelsea and England goalkeeper Reg Matthews signs for Derby County in October 1961, watched by chairman Harry Payne and manager Harry Storer. Matthews, a great character and a spectacular goalkeeper, was still playing for the Rams when Brian Clough took over as manager six years later. He made 246 League and Cup appearances for Derby.

In 1962, Harry Storer announced his retirement and the Rams appointed yet another former Derby and England player as manager, this time Tim Ward, the stylish wing-half whose career at the Baseball Ground began before World War Two. Tim Ward made 260 senior appearances for the Rams before being transferred to Barnsley in March 1951 to replace Danny Blanchflower. Ward is pictured at the Baseball Ground shortly after taking over.

Ken Oxford dives fearlessly at the feet of Leeds United's Jim Storrie in the goalless draw between the two clubs at the Baseball Ground in October 1962. The Rams ended the season in 18th place, five points clear of relegation to the Third Division. Leeds, on their way back to the top flight under Don Revie, ended the season in fifth place and were promoted as champions 12 months later.

Later in October 1962, high-flying Chelsea visited the Baseball Ground, where a 12,643 crowd saw Jack Parry score the Rams' goal in a 3-1 defeat by the London club who would end the season as Second Division runners-up under Tommy Docherty. Here, Bobby Tambling lets fly from the left wing. Derby players from left to right are Bobby Ferguson, Parry, Phil Waller and Geoff Barrowcliffe. Former Derby wing-half Frank Upton was playing for Chelsea.

In Tim Ward's first season as manager at the Baseball Ground the Rams started badly and this 3-1 win over Southampton in November was only their third from 17 games. Bobby Ferguson and Ken Oxford guard the goal-line as the Saints attack. The other Rams players are Phil Waller, Ray Young and Les Moore.

During the severe winter of 1962-63, football was badly affected and Derby did not play a League game between 22 December and 23 February. In the FA Cup they saw their third-round tie against Peterborough United postponed six times before Derby won 2-0 at the Baseball Ground on 4 February. They lost at Leyton Orient in the next round. Here, a Peterborough forward treads gingerly on the frozen surface but Jack Parry, coming in for the tackle, looks more sure-footed.

Sunderland goalkeeper Jim Montgomery punches clear from Rams forwards Barry Hutchinson and Johnny McCann at the Baseball Ground in October 1963. Rokerites defender Martin Harvey looks on. Derby lost to Sunderland 3-0 and the Wearsiders were promoted as runners-up.

Reg Matthews dives at the ball to thwart Crystal Palace centre-forward Derek Kevan at the Baseball Ground in November 1965. Also in the picture are Frank Upton (on ground), Bobby Saxton and Ron Webster. Derby, in their ninth game unbeaten, won 4-0.

With both teams on the fringe of the Second Division promotion race it was no surprise that Wolves' visit to the Baseball Ground in February 1966 attracted a crowd of over 27,000 who saw a 2-2 draw. Wolves goalkeeper Dave MacLaren pushes the ball around a post as Gordon Hughes closes in. Bobby Thomson is the Wolves defender. Eddie Thomas scored both Derby goals.

The team for the last home game of the 1965-66 season, a 1-0 win over Preston North End. Back row (left to right): Ron Webster, Phil Waller, Bobby Saxton, Reg Matthews, Frank Upton (who had rejoined the Rams from Chelsea in September 1965 and was substitute on this day), Peter Daniel, John Richardson, Billy Hodgson. Front row: Gordon Hughes, Eddie Thomas, Ian Buxton, Alan Durban (who scored the only goal of the game).

In September 1966 Derby County astonished their supporters by paying a club record transfer fee of £40,000 for the young Bradford striker Kevin Hector, who went on to appear in a record number of games for the Rams and who finished second only to the great Steve Bloomer in the list of the club's all-time scorers. Here, Hector signs watched by manager Tim Ward and chairman Sam Longson.

Reg Matthews flies through the air to clear from a Coventry City attack at the Baseball Ground in November 1966. Ron Webster and Bobby Saxton are close at hand. Coventry, the eventual Second Division champions, won 2-1 in front of a near-23,000 crowd.

Kevin Hector scored 201 goals for Derby County. Here is his sixth, a penalty blasted past Birmingham City goalkeeper Jim Herriot at the Baseball Ground in November 1966. But the Rams still lost, 2-1.

Derby County marked New Year's Eve 1966 with a 2-2 draw against Bolton Wanderers. Ian Buxton watches Alan Durban and Kevin Hector (8) challenge for the ball with Trotters' defenders John Napier (5) and Syd Farrimond (extreme right). The Rams ended the season in 17th place.

Kevin Hector gives Derby a fourth-minute lead by beating Cardiff City goalkeeper Bob Wilson from the penalty spot after Gareth Williams had tripped Alan Durban. This stormy game at the Baseball Ground in February 1967 finished 1-1.

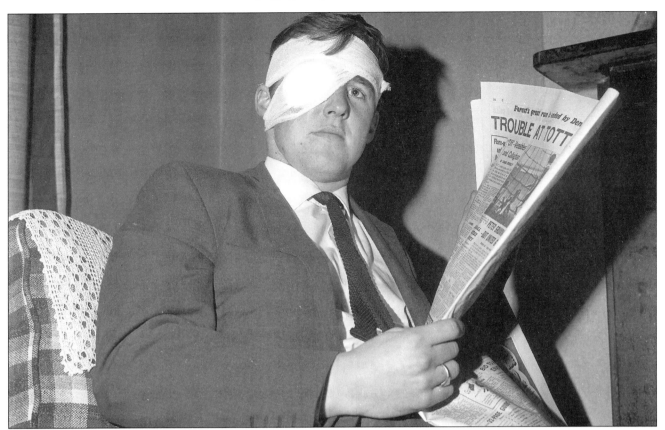

The day after the draw with Cardiff City in February 1967, Rams goalkeeper Colin Boulton is pictured at home nursing a badly cut eye after Cardiff's Greg Farrell's reckless challenge with Boulton already in charge of the ball. He left the field to have stitches inserted in the wound and Bobby Saxton took over in goal for a few minutes. Rams chairman Sam Longson criticised the referee for not dismissing Farrell, while after the match the Cardiff team bus was surrounded by angry Derby fans. Happily, Boulton recovered to play in the next League game.

The Derby County team that drew 1-1 with Plymouth Argyle at the Baseball Ground in May 1967. It was two days after Tim Ward had been sacked and a few weeks before Brian Clough and Peter Taylor arrived at the Baseball Ground. The team was selected by the Rams board, who asked Jack Parry to make his first appearance for 18 months. Parry declined, although he was listed as substitute. Back row (left to right): John Richardson, Peter Daniel, Colin Boulton, Bobby Saxton, Ron Webster, Phil Waller. Front row: Gordon Hughes, Derek Draper, Eddie Thomas, Ron Metcalfe (who was making the only League appearance of his career), Alan Durban.

Action from the 1-1 draw against Plymouth in the wake of Tim Ward's dismissal. Argyle goalkeeper Pat Dunne grabs a centre. Gordon Hughes and Eddie Thomas (9) are the Rams forwards. The Pilgrims' centre-half is John Newman (5), who later managed Derby County.

1 June 1967 and Rams chairman Sam Longson welcomes former England centre-forward Brian Clough to the Baseball Ground. Clough, recently in charge at Hartlepools United, is the Rams' new manager. His former Middlesbrough goalkeeping colleague Peter Taylor (left) is his assistant. Together they are about to take Derby County on a remarkable journey.

28 August 1967: a significant day for Derby County as Sam Longson welcomes 19-year-old centre-half Roy McFarland, a £24,000 signing by Clough from Tranmere Rovers. McFarland made his debut that evening, in a 3-1 win at Rotherham United, and began a career which was to last for 28 years - with an 18-month break - until 1995 when his contract as manager was not renewed.

John O'Hare (hidden), a signing from Sunderland, and Gordon Hughes challenge Aston Villa goalkeeper Colin Withers during a 3-1 win for the Rams at the Baseball Ground in September 1967. The players wore black armbands as a mark of respect to Harry Storer, a former player and manager, who had died the previous day.

On 16 September 1967, Derby beat Plymouth Argyle 1-0 to maintain their good start to the season (five wins and two defeats). Action here from the Rams' penalty area with Peter Daniel (2) and Roy McFarland (5) clearing the danger. Left to right are John Richardson, Bobby Saxton (who was transferred to Plymouth later that season), Norman Piper, Steve Davey, Daniel, McFarland, John Sillett, Ron Webster.

In October 1967, Derby beat Birmingham City 3-1 in the third round of the Football League Cup at the Baseball Ground. Bobby Saxton challenges Blues forward Geoff Vowden. The other Rams player is Ron Webster.

Three weeks after they had knocked Birmingham out of the League Cup, the Rams drew 2-2 with the Blues in a League game at the Baseball Ground. Birmingham goalkeeper Jim Herriot is beaten by a Rams goal attempt as full-back Colin Green waits on the line.

Blackburn goalkeeper Adam Blacklaw is beaten but Derby's Alan Durban and Rovers' Keith Newton watch as the ball goes wide at the Baseball Ground in late December 1968. The game ended 2-2.

January 1968 and a first taste of the great times that were ahead for Derby County as they reached the League Cup semi-final for the first time. Leeds United visited the Baseball Ground for the first leg and the Rams were doing well until Bobby Saxton inexplicably handled in the penalty area and Johnny Giles put away this spot-kick past Reg Matthews. Derby went down 1-0 and Saxton was soon on his way to Plymouth Argyle.

Rams forwards John O'Hare and Richie Barker challenge a Leeds defender for the ball. Almost 32,000 saw the first leg of the 1968 League Cup semi-final at the Baseball Ground. There were nearly 30,000 at Elland Road where Leeds completed a 4-2 aggregate victory.

On 2 March 1968 the Rams lost 3-2 at home to eventual Second Division champions Ipswich Town. Derby are attacking here with Kevin Hector trying to get in a header. The Ipswich defenders are Tommy Carroll and Bill Baxter.

29 July 1968: Dave Mackay, Tottenham Hotspur's great Scottish wing-half, has just signed for the Rams and young admirers crowd round for his autograph at the Municipal Sports Ground.

Derby on the defensive against Aston Villa at the Baseball Ground in September 1968. Mackay and young John Robson both appear to have missed the ball. Nearly 24,000 fans saw a 3-1 Derby win.

Cup fever hits town. In late September 1968, there were astonishing scenes at the Baseball Ground as fans queued for hours – some all night – and in pouring rain to buy tickets for the Football League Cup third-round replay against First Division Chelsea. Two days earlier the Rams had drawn 0-0 at Stamford Bridge.

The night that Derby County fans realised for certain that great times lay ahead. Dave Mackay and Roy McFarland defend heroically in the League Cup replay against Chelsea. A crowd of well over 34,000 saw a brilliant Rams performance as they won 3-1 with goals from Mackay, Durban and Hector.

Alan Durban gets in a shot despite the close attention of Chelsea's Eddie McCreadie.

Roy McFarland moves into the attack as Derby pour forward. Ron Harris and Kevin Hector look on as Chelsea goalkeeper Peter Bonetti prepares to block the shot.

Next up in the League Cup were another First Division outfit in the shape of Everton. Again the Rams drew 0-0 away from home before winning the replay, this time 1-0 with this goal from Kevin Hector who turns to crack the ball home.

Everton's Gordon West hurls himself at the ball as Hector closes in with John Hurst behind him.

Dave Mackay heads clear as the Merseysiders press for an equaliser. But the Rams defence held firm and they went into the fifth round. Alas, after all the previous dramas, this was a complete anticlimax, for they lost 1-0 in a replay at Third Division Swindon Town.

9 November 1968 and Willie Carlin, Jim Walker and John O'Hare celebrate the latter's goal in the 2-1 win over Charlton Athletic at the Baseball Ground. The Rams' fourth League win in succession.

2 December 1968: Brian Clough is pictured in his office at the Baseball Ground with his two-year-old son, Nigel. Clough, the proud father, has another reason to smile: the Rams have just beaten Crystal Palace to go top of the Second Division, where they remained for the rest of the season.

A spot of defending to do for Dave Mackay and Roy McFarland during the Rams' 4-2 win over Blackburn Rovers at the Baseball Ground on 1 March 1969. Don Martin is the Blackburn attacker, Ron Webster the Rams onlooker.

Promotion to Division One was achieved in style with a 5-1 win over Bolton Wanderers at the Baseball Ground in April 1969 as the Rams continued their remarkable end to the season, when they won their last nine games. Kevin Hector puts Derby ahead, lobbing Les Green's long kick over the head of Trotters' goalkeeper Eddie Hopkinson. In the background is the old Popular Side, soon to be overshadowed by the new Ley Stand.

John O'Hare takes Hector's pass to beat Hopkinson and put the Rams 3-1 ahead against Bolton.

Second-half action in the Bolton goalmouth as Frank Wignall heads goalwards. John O'Hare (9) is the other Rams forward; the Bolton players are (left to right) Syd Farrimond, Gareth Williams, Charlie Cooper, Arthur Marsh and goalkeeper Eddie Hopkinson. Alan Hinton is on the extreme right of the picture.

Promotion to the First Division was already assured when Derby County beat Sheffield United 1-0 with a goal from Alan Durban on Easter Monday 1969. The Blades' defenders are deflated as Durban (partly hidden) is congratulated by Kevin Hector and Roy McFarland. Willie Carlin (8) appears to be setting off on his own lap of honour.

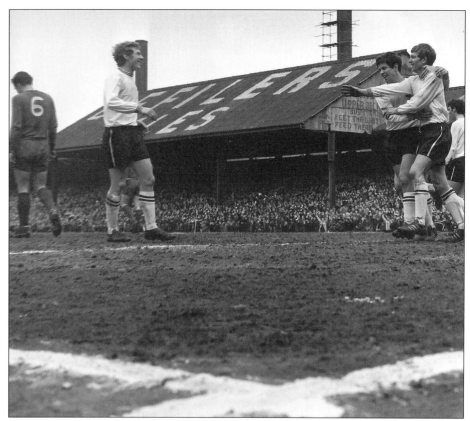

The Rams left the Second Division in style, beating Bristol City 5-0 at the Baseball Ground in their last League game of the remarkable 1968-69 season. Hat-trick hero Alan Durban is seen here accepting congratulations from Ron Webster and Alan Hinton. City's Gordon Parr trudges glumly away; Kevin Hector doesn't seem that happy either.

John O'Hare is blocked by Bristol City goalkeeper Barry Watling. Gordon Parr, Alec Briggs (3), Trevor Jacobs and Kevin Hector are also pictured.

Carnival time at the end of the game. Dave Mackay holds aloft the Second Division trophy as the rest of the Rams players accept the crowd's adulation. The Rams are back in the First Division after a glorious season, only their second under Brian Clough.

Derby County, Second Division champions 1968-69. Back row (left to right): Peter Taylor (assistant manager), Frank Wignall, John Robson, Ron Webster, Les Green, Roy McFarland, Alan Durban, Dave Mackay, Brian Clough (manager). Front row: Jim Walker, John McGovern, John O'Hare, Willie Carlin, Kevin Hector, Alan Hinton.

# The Seventies

## Two championship titles, glories in Europe, two winning managers sacked – and relegation just around the corner. Derby County were always national news.

On 20 September 1969 Derby County, back in the First Division, produced one of the most memorable performances in the club's history when, before a record Baseball Ground attendance of 41,826, they crushed Tottenham Hotspur 5-0. Pat Jennings is helpless to stop this Rams effort.

Kevin Hector, John O'Hare and Willie Carlin celebrate the latter's goal in the stunning victory over Spurs before a record crowd.

John O'Hare has just made it 5-0 and the rout of Spurs is complete. Willie Carlin, John McGovern and Kevin Hector race to congratulate the scorer. It was the Rams' fifth successive win on a wonderful return to the top flight.

4 October 1969: Derby's opening goal in their 2-0 victory over Manchester United before another 40,000 crowd at the Baseball Ground. Alex Stepney and John Fitzpatrick get into a tangle as Kevin Hector nods the ball goalwards. Francis Burns is also on the line and Willie Carlin lurks.

Future Rams hero Francis Lee (grounded) has just turned in Mike Summerbee's cross to give Manchester City a 1-0 victory at the Baseball Ground on 18 October 1969. Peter Daniel and Les Green appeal in vain for offside. The attendance was 40,788.

Rare action from the Derby penalty area during the 4-0 victory over Liverpool at the Baseball Ground on 1 November 1969. Les Green attempts to punch clear a Liverpool attack in the first half. From left to right are Roy McFarland, Alan Hinton, Ian St John, Peter Thompson, Dave Mackay, Chris Lawler, Green, Peter Daniel and Bobby Graham. A crowd of 40,993 saw yet another fantastic Rams performance.

John O'Hare, arm raised, celebrates Hector's great diving header in the 4-0 win over Liverpool in November 1969. Strong and Lawrence and the goalscorer lie in a heap and Lawler, Yeats and Hughes reflect on yet another Derby goal.

Derby put pressure on the Sunderland defence as Roy McFarland challenges goalkeeper Jim Montgomery with Alan Hinton and Willie Carlin looking on. The Rams beat the Wearsiders 3-0 at the Baseball Ground on 15 November 1969 before nearly 32,000 spectators.

Frank Wignall is on hand to congratulate John O'Hare, who has just scored one of his goals in a 2-0 win over West Bromwich Albion at the Baseball Ground just after Christmas 1969.

After a heavy snowfall in early January 1970, Rams manager Brian Clough lends a hand to clear the Baseball Ground pitch in readiness for the FA Cup third-round replay against Preston North End. The match went ahead and Derby won 4-1.

Six minutes remaining in the First Division match between Derby County and Sheffield Wednesday at the Baseball Ground in January 1970, John O'Hare and Sam Ellis each look determined to get to the ball after goalkeeper Springett had blocked Alan Durban's effort. O'Hare won, just managing to push it past Springett for the only goal of the game.

When Terry Hennessey joined Derby County in February 1970, from Nottingham Forest, he became the Rams' first £100,000 signing. Here Hennessey, a Welsh international wing-half, is pictured with Dave Mackay and Roy McFarland at the Municipal Sports Ground. Both Mackay and McFarland would go on to manage the Rams. Injury would bring a premature end to Hennessey's playing career.

Kevin Hector receives congratulations following his goal, the Rams' second, against Arsenal at the Baseball Ground in February 1970. Derby won 3-2 in front of more than 35,000 spectators. Hector is number 10, O'Hare is mostly hidden, Durban is number 7, then Hinton. Carlin (8) looks thoughtful. George Graham, later to manage the Gunners and then end up disgraced, looks from afar, hands on hips.

The letter which Derby County dreaded. In April 1970, a postman arrives at the front door of the Baseball Ground with a letter from the Football Association which contained news of the club's fate following an enquiry into financial irregularities at the Baseball Ground. The Rams had just finished fourth in Division One and were eagerly anticipating a place in European competition the following season. A £10,000 fine was bad enough, but the FA also banned the Rams from Europe for a year. It was a bitter blow. And it wouldn't be the last time that Derby County's name was making headlines for off-the-field activities.

In August 1970, Derby County beat Manchester United in the Watney Cup, a sponsored pre-season tournament which tried out an experimental offside law. Despite the low-key nature of the competition it attracted big crowds for the Rams: over 18,500 for the first round at Fulham, over 25,000 for the home semi-final against Sheffield United and a remarkable 32,000 for the Final against Manchester United at the Baseball Ground. The Rams beat United 4-1. This picture shows action from the United goalmouth with Roy McFarland and Willie Carlin the nearest Rams players and Kevin Hector looking on. United's defenders all look disconsolate but the crowd aren't in celebratory mood. In fact, the linesman's flag was just going up for offside.

The Rams line up with the Watney Cup and their individual awards. Back row (left to right): Dave Mackay, Ron Webster (hidden), John McGovern, Alan Hinton (behind the trophy), John O'Hare, John Robson, Les Green and Willie Carlin. Front row: Alan Durban, Kevin Hector and Roy McFarland.

Alan Hinton blasts a penalty past Tottenham Hotspur goalkeeper Pat Jennings at the Baseball Ground in October 1970. Hinton's spot-kick earned Derby a 1-1 draw. Over 36,000 people saw the game.

Goalmouth action from the goalless draw against Liverpool at the Baseball Ground in November 1970. Players (left to right) are Emlyn Hughes, Brian Hall, Roy McFarland, Ray Clemence, Alan Durban, John O'Hare, Larry Lloyd and Kevin Hector. The crowd was over 33,000.

In February 1971, Derby awoke to find that the unthinkable had happened – Rolls-Royce, the town's 'job for life' employer, was bankrupt. Brian Clough soon took people's minds of their immediate troubles, though. He went out and paid a British record £170,000 for a defender when he signed Colin Todd from Sunderland. Here, Todd, newly-arrived in Derby, signs a football for a supporter in Shaftesbury Crescent. Note the terraced houses which were later demolished and which space now provides parking for official's cars.

27 February 1971: the Gunners defenders blame each other as Derby celebrate a Roy McFarland goal in a 2-0 Rams victory over Arsenal at the Baseball Ground before 35,775 spectators. Players (left to right) are Bob McNab, Frank McLintock, John Radford, Bob Wilson, Charlie George (later to become a great Derby favourite), McFarland, John O'Hare and John McGovern.

John O'Hare gets in between Everton defenders Howard Kendall and Tommy Wright in scoring one of his two goals in the Rams' 3-1 victory at the Baseball Ground in April 1971.

4 December 1971: Ron Webster, who began his Derby County career when Harry Storer managed the club, heads home his first goal since October 1966. It helped the Rams to beat Manchester City 3-1 at the Baseball Ground during their first League championship-winning season.

Kevin Hector, arms aloft, has just scored and Nottingham Forest are in tatters during Derby's 4-0 home win on 19 February 1972. The championship is still two months or more away and this was the first in a string of five consecutive victories. Left to right are Sammy Chapman, Alan Hinton, Hector, John Winfield, Jim Barron, Peter Hindley and John O'Hare.

In 1971-72, Derby County joined battle with Arsenal in what turned out to be an epic FA Cup fifth-round tie. The sides first drew 2-2 at the Baseball Ground in front of 39,622 spectators and then a remarkable 63,077 saw the Highbury replay on a Wednesday afternoon – most floodlit football was banned during a major industrial dispute which caused thousands of power cuts across Britain. Eventually, Arsenal won 1-0 at Filbert Street in a second replay. This picture shows Alan Durban heading an 88th-minute equaliser in the first game after the Rams had trailed to two Charlie George goals. Bob Wilson is the goalkeeper, Sammy Nelson and Peter Simpson the equally helpless defenders.

4 March 1972: Derby County controversially parade Nottingham Forest winger Ian Storey-Moore as their 'new signing' before the home game against Wolves. But the Forest committee objected to the player moving just down the road and he eventually went to Manchester United, leaving Derby County with egg on their faces. Storey-Moore acknowledges the crowd flanked by assistant manager Peter Taylor and club secretary Stuart Webb.

Alan Hinton beats Wolves goalkeeper Phil Parkes at the Baseball Ground in the Rams' 2-1 win in March 1972. Roy McFarland scored the other Derby goal. A crowd of 33,456 saw the game.

1 April 1972: a crucial game against League championship rivals Leeds United at the Baseball Ground. John O'Hare hits in a left-foot shot watched by (from left to right) Terry Cooper, Ron Webster, Johnny Giles and Allan Clarke. Derby won two important points with a 2-0 win, their goals coming from O'Hare and a Norman Hunter own-goal.

In the same vital game against Leeds, Jim Walker hammers in a goalbound shot only to see Paul Reaney clear off the line.
Left to right are John McGovern, Walker, Johnny Giles, Roy McFarland, Paul Madeley, Jack Charlton and John Robson. Jim
Walker is currently the first-team physiotherapist at Aston Villa.

Rams players celebrate John O'Hare's goal as Leeds goalkeeper Gary Sprake looks crestfallen. This performance confirmed
the belief that Derby County could indeed go all the way in the championship race.

In late April 1972 the Rams met Airdrie in the delayed second leg of the Texaco Cup Final. The sides had drawn 0-0 in Scotland in January. Now over 25,000 fans saw the Rams lift the sponsored trophy 2-1 at the Baseball Ground. (Left) Early in the game, Airdrie goalkeeper McKenzie tips over a header from Kevin Hector. (Right) Roger Davies nods Barry Butlin's centre past McKenzie for the Rams' second goal.

Back to the serious stuff: the game that won the Football League championship, although the Rams did not know it at the time. On 1 May 1972, Derby beat Liverpool 1-0 at the Baseball Ground in front of 39,159 fans. That left them top of the table but they flew off on holiday with the knowledge that both Liverpool and Leeds United, who still had games to play, could overtake them. Both failed, though, and a glorious night of celebrations in Derby began one week after this famous victory over Liverpool. Roy McFarland, Chris Lawler, Steve Powell (still only 16), Larry Lloyd, Colin Todd and John Robson battle it out.

The goal that won a championship. John McGovern, a £7,000 signing from Hartlepool United, falls as he hits the winning goal against Liverpool on 1 May 1972.

9 May 1972: the morning after both Leeds and Liverpool failed to gain the results that would have given one or the other of them the title. Instead Derby County are League champions for the first time in the club's 88-year history. At the Baseball Ground, directors open the bubbly. The old floodlights still perch atop the double-decker stands at each end of the ground. Soon they will give way to lighting from pylons, strong enough for good colour television pictures. The Rams, of course, are now in the European Cup.

Young supporters of both teams rush to congratulate their heroes after Derby's win over Liverpool. Colin Todd and Tommy Smith exchange a handshake; Roy McFarland watches as Brian Hall meets a fan. It's all over now, bar the waiting.

Because they were in Majorca when confirmed as champions, when they arrived back in England on the following Sunday morning, the Rams made plans to go straight from the East Midlands Airport to the Baseball Ground, where thousands of supporters saw them presented with the Football League championship trophy. They also show off the Central League championship trophy and the Texaco Cup.

In September 1972, when the Rams beat Liverpool 2-1 at the Baseball Ground, their equalising goal was a controversial affair. Alan Hinton swung over a harmless-looking centre and as the ball dropped towards the crossbar Liverpool goalkeeper Frankie Lane, who was making his debut in place of the injured Ray Clemence, caught it under the bar. The linesman signalled goal, although as these photographs show, he was hardly best placed. Needless to say, Liverpool weren't best-pleased, either. In the first picture Lane catches the ball as Hector waits; in the second Hector and and the crowd are celebrating but the linesman is hardly in line. An 87th-minute goal from John O'Hare finished the job.

16 September 1972: another home win for Derby County, this time 1-0 against Birmingham City. Steve Powell, still four days short of 17th birthday, starts his eighth League match. Like his father, Tommy Powell, Steve would become a wonderful servant to his only League club.

14 October 1972: Terry Hennessey, who scored Derby's winning goal in their 2-1 victory over Leicester City at the Baseball Ground, watches as Leicester goalkeeper Peter Shilton gathers the ball. Graham Cross is the Leicester defender. By the following spring, Hennessey's playing career was over, finished by injuries; Shilton, however, who played for the Rams from 1987 to 1992, would still be playing almost a quarter of a century later.

25 October 1972: European Cup action against Benfica at the Baseball Ground. In one of the greatest and most passionate nights that the old ground has ever seen, the Rams beat the Portuguese champions 3-0. Roy McFarland surges in to head Alan Hinton's corner past José Henriques for the first goal.

Terry Hennessey is left open-mouthed as the Benfica goal escapes. Kevin Hector and John McGovern completed the scoring in front of 38,100 fans and in Lisbon the Rams gained a goalless draw.

Arsenal goalkeeper Bob Wilson is helpless as Kevin Hector heads home Derby County's third goal in their 5-0 demolition of the Gunners at the Baseball Ground in November 1972. Peter Simpson, Frank McLintock, Roger Davies (making his home debut) and Terry Hennessey look on.

The Rams find the net again as Arsenal are routed. Roy McFarland (5) takes off in delight; Archie Gemmill also celebrates; the goalscorer is hidden behind two Arsenal defenders.

Roger Davies shields the ball from Peter Simpson. The other Arsenal player is Eddie Kelly. Over 31,000 saw this fine Rams victory.

John O'Hare fires in an effort towards the Leeds United goal at the Baseball Ground on 3 March 1973. Norman Hunter, not normally known for a faint heart, takes evasive action. In a fiery encounter – and in those days Derby-Leeds matches were often ill-tempered affairs – the Rams lost 3-2. Referee Ron Challis awarded two controversial penalties to Leeds. Afterwards Mr Challis' face came into contact with Colin Boulton's muddy glove. The goalkeeper was later suspended for two matches.

21 March 1973: Derby trailed 1-0 from the first leg of their European Cup quarter-final against the Czech champions Spartak Trnava. At the Baseball Ground they won 2-0 to go through, although the last half-hour was tense. One goal from the Czechs would have swung the tie their way. Hector (partly hidden) scores his first goal to level the scores on aggregate. He netted again later.

Derby County's European Cup dream ended when Juventus earned a goalless draw at the Baseball Ground on 25 April 1973. It wa[s] an awful night for Rams fans with Alan Hinton missing a penalty and Roger Davies being sent off. Here Dino Zoff, the Italians' great international 'keeper, scrambles across his goal to deny the Rams yet again.

Roger Davies is led off by Rams trainer Jimmy Gordon. Davies suffered a rush of blood in the Normanton goalmouth, tang with Zoff and was shown the red card.

October 1973: a storm breaks over the Baseball Ground, the like of which had never been seen before – or since – in football. Brian Clough and Peter Taylor have just resigned. The Rams board, particularly chairman Sam Longson, did not like Clough's high profile as a media celebrity and an outspoken one at that. The game's authorities warned Longson – "Keep your manager under control." Longson couldn't, so he emptied the manager's drinks cabinet and when Clough couldn't find anything suitable to toast a victory at Old Trafford, he took the hint and chucked in his job. Players and supporters alike were appalled. Here, a sombre Clough and Taylor speak to the Press.

Derby County's players threatened strike action if Clough was not reinstated. Alan Hinton does his Neville Chamberlain impression, presumably with a petition demanding Clough's return; Colin Boulton and Ron Webster look amused, slightly embarrassed even. After all, it is not often that footballers become militants.

98gation">*IMAGES OF DERBY COUNTY*

Clough wasn't coming back, of course. Instead the Derby board appointed former playing favourite Dave Mackay as the new manager. Roy McFarland implored Mackay not to take the job but he is no quitter. He came back to Derby facing a difficult situation but, typically, attacked it head on. Here, Mackay pins up his first team sheet as Derby County's manager.

Mackay faces the Press in his first week as Rams boss. His assistant, Des Anderson, looks on.

In 1955, Derby County were the victims of an FA Cup sensation, losing 6-1 at home to Boston United, who included six Rams 'old boys'. In January 1974, Boston were drawn at the Baseball Ground again. This time the scoreline was goalless, still a surprise but not a disaster. In the replay at York Street the Rams laid the ghost of 19 years earlier, winning by an identical scoreline. Here, Peter Daniel and Jeff Bourne go up for the ball in the Boston goalmouth at the Baseball Ground. Rod Thomas is the other Derby player. Phil Waller, formerly of Derby County, was in the Boston line-up.

21 February 1974: Rams manager Dave Mackay with his new signing Bruce Rioch, who cost £200,000 from Aston Villa. Rioch, a goalscoring midfielder, was a major factor in Derby regaining the League title the following year. He also captained Scotland, the first Englishman to do so (he was born in Aldershot of a Scottish father). And he later made a name for himself as a manager, although in February 1995 he did not endear himself to a new generation of Derby fans following remarks after his Bolton Wanderers team had visited the Baseball Ground.

23 March 1974: consternation in the Derby County goalmouth during the 2-0 win over Ipswich Town. Left to right are Kevin Beattie (6), Trevor Whymark, Roy McFarland (diving to head clear), Clive Woods, Colin Boulton, Eric Gates, David Nish and Rod Thomas.

Derby County launched their fund-raising 'Baseball Bonanza' in 1974. Roger Davies, Jeff Bourne, Colin Boulton and Francis Lee are pictured with a giant ticket. Still, £300 was a lot of money in those days.

18 September 1974: Colin Boulton fists out the ball from an attack by the Swiss club Servette during a UEFA Cup-tie at the Baseball Ground. Henry Newton, Peter Daniel, Colin Todd and Archie Gemmill (8) are in support. The Rams beat Servette 4-1 on the night and 6-2 on aggregate. Less than 18,000 bothered to turn out.

23 November 1974: Kevin Hector heads home the Rams' second goal in their 2-0 win over Ipswich Town. Laurie Sivell is the Town goalkeeper, Francis Lee and Roger Davies the other Rams players. Mick Mills is behind Lee. Town's right-back is George Burley, their manager in 1995.

Bruce Rioch blasts home a penalty against Bristol Rovers in the fourth round of the FA Cup at the Baseball Ground in January 1975. Rioch, who places his spot-kick perfectly past Rovers goalkeeper Jim Eadie, scored 20 goals in all competitions that season, remarkable for a midfielder. Derby won 2-0 but lost at home to Leeds, 1-0, in the next round.

As we have noted earlier, in the early 1970s games between Derby County and Leeds United were often highlighted by bad temper. Things were no different on 8 February 1975 when the goalless draw between the sides at the Baseball Ground saw violence again simmer. Paul Reaney tries to get between goalkeeper David Harvey and Rams striker Francis Lee. For Lee it was a taste of what was to come nine months later when Leeds again visited the Baseball Ground.

29 March 1975 was definitely Roger Davies' day. The big striker, signed from non-League football by Brian Clough, scored all the goals as Luton Town were beaten 5-0 at the Baseball Ground, setting up a profitable Easter for Derby, who took maximum points from their three holiday games. Here, Davies leaps high to head home Hinton's cross for his opening goal. Peter Daniel is the other Rams player. To the left is Paul Futcher, who was to play for Derby County eight years later, and Futcher's twin brother Ron (9).

Left: Hatters' goalkeeper Keith Barber can do nothing to prevent Davies' second goal, a header from Rod Thomas' centre.

More danger for Luton as Davies chips the ball towards Barber's goal once more.

It might have been more. One of Davies' two disallowed goals, a diving header ruled out for offside. Steve Buckley looks on. Buckley eventually found his way to the Baseball Ground via Ilkeston Town, Burton Albion and Luton. He cost £163,000 and repaid the Rams with 366 senior appearances. They could have had him for nothing, though. When the Rams were winning their first League championship, Buckley was playing for Redfern Athletic in Derby Sunday football.

It is April 1975, heady days of spring for Derby County who are on the verge of a second League championship. One man has missed most of the season, though. Roy McFarland was injured playing for England at Wembley 11 months earlier and his Achilles tendon so badly damaged that at one time his very career was in doubt. Unsung reserve Peter Daniel, a Ripley lad signed by Tim Ward in 1963, took over at centre-half and performed magnificently week after week. He was courageous, too, often playing with pain-killing drugs to help him through with a bad pelvic strain. On 9 April, Wolves visited the Baseball Ground and McFarland returned. Daniel moved to left-back (Nish was injured) but he retained the number-five shirt he had graced all season. The Rams won 1-0 and here we see McFarland leaving the field and Daniel waiting for him. The following week McFarland was back in the number-five shirt, Nish was back, too, and 'Ticker' Daniel took a well-earned rest, his job done to perfection.

Derby County were unbeaten in their last nine League games of 1974-75 to win the League championship again. And if the final game of the season, a goalless draw against Carlisle United, was hardly a highlight, the fact that the Rams could parade the League trophy certainly made up for it. Colin Boulton, the only man to be ever-present in both championship-winning seasons, holds the trophy with help from Roger Davies. Kevin Hector admires Bruce Rioch's award.

Earlier, the teams had fought out a 0-0 draw. Roger Davies sends a header over the Cumbrians' crossbar.

Civic processions were becoming a regular occurrence. First 1969 and promotion celebrations, then 1972 and the championship. Now 1975 and another title to herald. Not so many people as the time that Derby County won the FA Cup in 1946, perhaps, but still a fair sized crowd to see the Rams' bus thread its way towards the Council House. In the background, work continues on the new Assembly Rooms. The infamous 'Hole' has yet to be excavated; the Market Place water feature yet to be dreamed up. The time by the Guildhall clock is five minutes to eight on a late spring evening.

July 1975 and Dave Mackay's new signing Charlie George reports for training at the Raynesway ground. George appears to be praying for a good season. Francis Lee probably had far greater business matters on his mind.

Action in front of the Ipswich Town goal at the Baseball Ground in October 1975, but there seems little danger judging by the position of the ball. Roy McFarland is trying to pose a threat to Cooper's goal. Trevor Whymark, who later played briefly for Derby, is next to him. Hunter and Mills are the other Ipswich players nearest the camera; Eric Gates is in the distance.

22 October 1975 was a night when Derby County glittered. Real Madrid, the greatest name in the rich history of the European Cup, were destroyed 4-1 at the Baseball Ground. Charlie George gives the Rams the lead with his 'wonder goal'. Unfortunately there was the little matter of the second leg.

Charlie George beats Real Madrid's goalkeeper Miguel from the penalty spot to complete his hat-trick and the Rams' scoring.

At the other end goalkeeper Colin Boulton cannot hide his delight as the Rams cap another superb performance. And why should he?

What a difference two weeks make. In Madrid, the Rams went down 5-1 to lose the European Cup tie on aggregate. Yet they were only five minutes from safety when Rod Thomas gave away a penalty to ensure extra-time. Charlie George walks across the tarmac at the East Midlands Airport upon the Rams' return. His hat-trick against the Spanish champions two weeks earlier means little now.

1 November 1975: the day the tinderbox finally exploded. Three minutes from half-time against Leeds United at the Baseball Ground with the match poised at 1-1, Francis Lee won a penalty after bustling past Norman Hunter. Charlie George sends David Harvey the wrong way. Derby finally emerged 3-2 winners, but not before Hunter and Lee had settled some old scores.

Seven minutes after the interval, the Derby-Leeds game boiled over. Hunter, still annoyed about the penalty, clattered Lee, who retaliated. Hunter's fist then came into contact with Lee's lip, which required four stitches. Referee Derek Nippard sent both men off. On the way to the dressing-room they began again and wholesale fighting broke out with over ten players involved one way or the other. Billy Bremner and Archie Gemmill are particularly keen to have a go, and David Harvey is a long way from his goal. Today, such scenes would surely result in serious punishment, perhaps the clubs each having points deducted.

A blood-splattered Francis Lee is led away by Rams trainer Gordon Guthrie with a grim-faced Dave Mackay and Des Anderson behind. Lee was later fined £200 by the FA and suspended for four games. Remarkably, Hunter got away with no punishment at all.

A superb goal late in the game from substitute Roger Davies gave the Rams victory over Leeds and reminded supporters that it was football they had come to see. Here Davies (out of picture) gives David Harvey no chance with a swerving left-foot shot into the far corner. Charlie George and Paul Reaney admire the glorious effort.

Derby County threatened to retain the League championship in 1975-76, but the calendar year of 1975 was probably their peak, when they lost only eight out of 42 League matches from 11 January to 27 December. When Aston Villa came to the Baseball Ground for the final game of the year, the Rams won 2-0, helped by this headed goal from Steve Powell. John Gidman and Charlie George are also airborne. Derby had last led the table in early December and eventually they finished fourth, seven points behind champions Liverpool.

Liverpool may have beaten Derby to the title in 1975-76 but the Rams knocked the Merseysiders out of the FA Cup at the Baseball Ground, winning 1-0 in the fourth round with a goal from Roger Davies before 38,000 fans. It was this close-range effort from Davies which took the Rams through. Davies has just come on as substitute and was earning a reputation as a so-called 'super sub'. Francis Lee looks pleased. Understandably, Emlyn Hughes, Phil Neal, Ray Clemence and company do not share his joy.

The fifth round of the 1975-76 FA Cup saw the Rams drawn at home to Third Division Southend United. The Essex club provided tough opposition and the only time their defence was breached was when Bruce Rioch (4) hammered home this left-foot rocket of a shot.

The FA Cup quarter-final against Newcastle United saw a brilliant Rams display to win 4-2. Bruce Rioch (out of picture) cracks a perfect free-kick into the top corner of Edgar's net.

Another view of Rioch's free-kick with Newcastle 'keeper Edgar beaten in the most classic style.

Charlie George tucks away Derby's fourth goal against Newcastle United in the 1976 FA Cup quarter-final. Alas, George was injured in the League match against Stoke at the Baseball Ground just over two weeks later and apart from him missing the Cup semi-final, his absence almost certainly cost the Rams dear in the League.

In April 1976, Derby County met Manchester United in an FA Cup semi-final at Hillsborough. Thirty-eight years earlier, their last semi-final appearance was against the same opponents on the same ground. Unfortunately, the result was the same, too, the Rams losing both games by two goals. On the eve of the semi-final, Derby County players leave the Baseball Ground for Sheffield. Colin Todd and Bruce Rioch – later to forge a successful managerial pairing – board the coach followed by Kevin Hector.

28 August 1976 and Manchester United draw 0-0 at the Baseball Ground. Derby appeal for a penalty as Charlie George (nearest to the referee) is accompanied by Eric Carruthers, seen here on his only first-team appearance for the Rams, as a substitute, following his £15,000 move from Heart of Midlothian. This game was marred by a major pitch invasion by rival supporters. It was 16 October before the Rams won a game – incredibly, when they did it was 8-2 against Spurs – and soon people were calling for the removal of manager Dave Mackay. Remarkable considering Derby's League positions since he took over – third, first and fourth and a Cup semi-final.

15 September 1976: Derby County recorded their biggest-ever win with a 12-0 thrashing of Finn Harps at the Baseball Ground in the UEFA Cup first-round first-leg tie. Kevin Hector hit the Irish part-timers for five goals, Charlie George and Leighton James each scored a hat-trick. The Rams won the second leg 4-1. Here Charlie George heads goalwards at Derby.

Kevin Hector scores one of his five goals, slipping the ball past Harps goalkeeper Murray. The game attracted only 13,353 spectators.

Charlie George thunders in a shot to make it 5-0 against Finn Harps, Four more goals were added before half-time.

25 September 1976: it's all West Brom defenders at the Baseball Ground but it's Derby County who have scored. Roy McFarland has just netted one of his goals in the 2-2 draw. John Wile and goalkeeper John Osborne look at each other. Joe Mayo and Paddy Mulligan trudge back to restart the game. The Albion player adjusting his sock in the back of the net is future England captain Bryan Robson.

16 October 1976: Bruce Rioch is first to the ball to steer it past Tottenham goalkeeper Pat Jennings for his second goal during the 8-2 thrashing of Spurs at the Baseball Ground.

As Derby pin Spurs back with wave after wave of attacking football, Charlie George attempts to 'lob' Pat Jennings.

George makes it 6-2 from the penalty spot, sending Jennings the wrong way after Steve Perryman had tripped Archie Gemmill.

The evening of 3 November 1976 saw Derby County play in top-class European competition for the last time to date. Trailing 2-0 from the first leg of this UEFA Cup-tie against AEK Athens, the Rams went down 3-2 at the Baseball Ground. Goalkeeper Stergiousis is pictured punching clear with Charlie George in close attendance.

Dave Mackay, angered by criticism of his management style, asked the Rams board for a vote of confidence. After much shuffling of feet, nervous coughing and skyward stares, he wasn't given one and in November 1976 he was sacked. Chairman Sam Longson, who in four years had got rid of two managers who won the League championship for Derby County, greets the new man Colin Murphy, who had been coaching the Rams reserve team.

Colin Murphy and Stuart Webb look pleased to have signed Charlton Athletic striker Derek Hales for £330,000 in December 1976. Alas, no one at the Baseball Ground was smiling after Hales, having failed at Derby, was transferred to West Ham at a huge financial loss to the Rams, although one local scribe still chuckles at the time he described Hales as 'the new Gerd Müller'.

The Rams managed another good FA Cup run in Colin Murphy's season as manager, reaching the quarter-finals before losing 2-0 at Goodison Park. In the third round Derby beat Blackpool 3-2 in a Baseball Ground replay on 19 January 1977. Leighton James slots their second goal past the Seasiders' goalkeeper George Wood. Derby's Tony Macken looks on.

22 February 1977: Brian Clough returns to the Baseball Ground, courted by new chairman George Hardy to become manager again. Derby County supporters always hoped he would come back and many crowded outside to implore him. But Forest would not release him from his contract and an unhappy Clough has to say, "Thanks, but no thanks." Typically, though, he chose to do it with a media circus in attendance.

15 April 1977: Ron Webster is about to equal Derby County's appearance record when he plays in his 525th senior game for the Rams against Everton the following day. Webster was enjoying a run at left-back, preferred to Rod Thomas (who had replaced him two years earlier) when injuries to David Nish and Peter Daniel gave him the chance to break the record. Webster eventually signed off with 535 senior appearances for the Rams, only five of them coming as a substitute.

Manchester City were 'on a roll' and chasing the League championship when a struggling Derby County side thumped them 4-0 at the Baseball Ground in April 1977, even though the Rams were badly hit by injuries. Archie Gemmill hits his only goal of the season with this left-footed drive.

Peter Daniel lunges to turn David Langan's cross past Joe Corrigan: 2-0 to Derby County. Nearly 30,000 saw Manchester City humbled. The Rams ended the season in 15th place. City failed to catch champions Nottingham Forest, finishing 12 points behind the leaders.

This was the real reason why Manchester City's visit in April 1977 was so memorable, though – the now legendary penalty spot fiasco. The spot disappeared in the Baseball Ground mud and when the Rams were awarded a penalty, referee John Yates called for a tape measure. He finds the spot while City goalkeeper Joe Corrigan gives groundsman Bob Smith a helping hand with the brush and whitewash.

After all the farce, Gerry Daly fires home the penalty to put the Rams 4-0 ahead, easily the best result of Colin Murphy's short reign as Derby County manager.

Derby pulled clear of the relegation zone under Murphy, losing only twice in their last 17 games of 1976-77 after being bottom of the table on 5 March. On 11 May, in their penultimate game of the season, they beat Queen's Park Rangers 2-0 at the Baseball Ground. Charlie George receives treatment from trainer Gordon Guthrie. Referee George Courtney looks on; Leighton James seems amused.

24 August 1977: Derek Hales gets in a shot during one of his last appearances for Derby County, against Ipswich Town at the Baseball Ground, a game which ended goalless. A few weeks later Colin Murphy was replaced by Tommy Docherty, who never selected Hales. Indeed, the big striker was sold to West Ham within a fortnight for £110,000; Derby had recently paid £330,000 for him.

Former Sunderland forward Billy Hughes heads the ball past Norwich City goalkeeper Kevin Keelan at the Baseball Ground in October 1977. The result was 2-2. Hughes, who later ran a pub in Derby, was the Rams leading scorer when, in December 1977, Tommy Docherty inexplicably sold him to Leicester City. But then players moved in and out of the Baseball Ground at a bewildering rate under Docherty's stewardship.

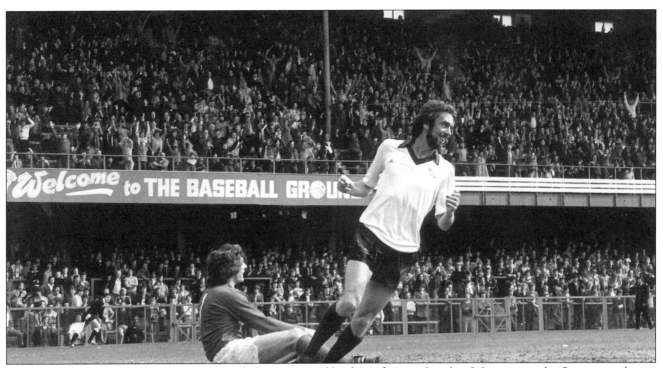

Arsenal goalkeeper Pat Jennings is grounded as Steve Buckley (out of camera) seals a 2-0 won over the Gunners at the Baseball Ground in April 1979. Roy Greenwood is the delighted Rams forward. Derby County had struggled in Docherty's second season of turmoil and this was one of only two wins in their final 19 games of 1978-79. They escaped relegation and on the eve of the FA Cup Final, Docherty was on his way to manage QPR. Few at Derby mourned his going.

# The Eighties

## From First Division to Third, the Rams' fortunes tumbled. Even the club's very existence was in doubt. But their future was secured, Arthur Cox arrived and the reverse journey began.

New manager Colin Addison found that Tommy Docherty's buying and selling spree at the Baseball Ground had left Derby County in an unstable condition. The glory days were over and there were now many more dark days than highlights, more defeats than victories. On 20 October 1979 the Rams lost 3-1 to Aston Villa at the Baseball Ground before 20,000 fans. Paul Emson, raises his hands in glee after scoring the Rams' goal. Vic Moreland and Roger Davies, who had returned to the club the previous month, offer congratulations.

Rams chairman George Hardy with new manager Colin Addison, formerly boss at Newport County and Hereford United and later Ron Atkinson's assistant at West Brom. Addison had a bizarre start to his Derby County career. Hardy, the man who appointed him, was ousted before the season began and, entirely unconnected with Hardy's departure, the club was the subject of a police investigation into alleged financial irregularities.

Derby County ended the 1979-80 season with relegation to Division Two, from where they had re-emerged so triumphantly under Brian Clough ten years earlier. But there was one delicious moment for Rams fans. It came on 24 November 1979 in the shape of a 4-1 defeat over bitter rivals Nottingham Forest at the Baseball Ground. The Rams celebrate Gerry Daly's opening goal. Left to right are David Webb, Keith Osgood, Roger Davies, Daly and Barry Powell. Addison struggled with injuries to key players and Daly, McFarland, Duncan and Steve Powell all missed big chunks of the season.

Goalmouth action against Forest. John Duncan, Larry Lloyd, Dave Needham and Steve Emery are at sixes and sevens.

Barry Powell heads home Alan Biley's cross past Manchester United goalkeeper Gary Bailey to give Derby the lead at the Baseball Ground on 2 February 1980. Unfortunately, Powell also put through his own goal as United scored twice in second-half injury time to win 3-1.

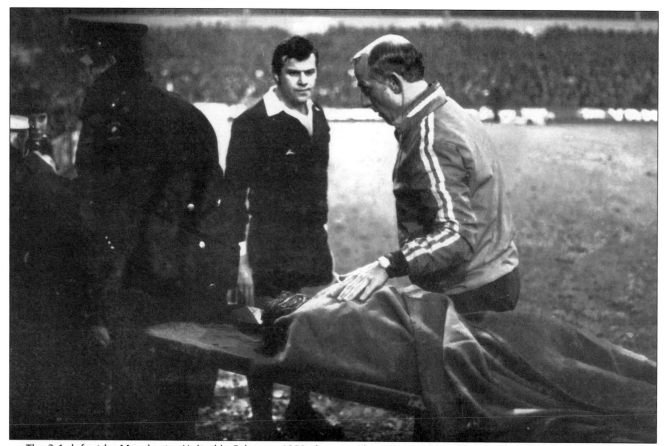

The 3-1 defeat by Manchester United in February 1980 also saw Alan Biley carried off on a stretcher after clashing with Gordon McQueen. Trainer Gordon Guthrie looks worried and, indeed, Biley, a £300,000 signing from Cambridge United, did not regain consciousness until he was in the dressing-room. Happily he recovered and played in all the remaining games of the season as the Rams battled vainly to avoid the drop.

23 February 1980 and Derby's first win in three months. Alan Biley dives to head his first goal for the club past Tottenham's Mark Kendall. The Rams won 2-1 and Biley ended the season as the division's joint second-highest scorer with 21 goals (if one counts the 12 he scored for Cambridge). Top scorer, with 23, was Southampton's Phil Boyer, released by Brian Clough in 1968 without ever playing in the Rams' first team.

The Rams made a good start to their first season back in Division Two and were second in the table by mid-September. Early in the month they came from 2-0 down to draw with leaders Blackburn Rovers at the Baseball Ground, both goals coming from Alan Biley, who celebrates this one watched by Kevin Wilson.

April 1981 and the Rams, on their way to finishing in sixth place, having lost their mid-season form, led Notts County 2-0 at the Baseball Ground but were held to a 2-2 draw in the end. Keith Osgood scores from the penalty spot. To the horror of Derby fans, the Magpies were promoted to the First Division at the end of the season, eight points ahead of the Rams.

In 1981-82 the Rams began to struggle. In late October, Dave Swindlehurst, who cost a club record £400,000 from Crystal Palace, watches former Derby reserve goalkeeper Nigel Batch make a save for Grimsby Town at the Baseball Ground. The Rams led by a John Clayton goal but were stunned deep into injury time by a speculative effort from Mick Brolly, later to play for Derby, which squared the match.

As the depressing 1981-82 season drew to a close, a crowd of just over 10,000 saw Cardiff City gain a goalless draw at the Baseball Ground in May. Dave Swindlehurst has been thwarted by the Bluebirds' goalkeeper Ron Healey. Parts of the Ley Stand are empty, a far cry from the days when attendances of 40,000 were not that unusual.

Although the Rams finished in 16th place in Division Two in 1981-82, when the last day of the season arrived they were still not sure of staying up. John Newman, Colin Addison's assistant, had replaced his boss as Derby manager after Christmas and now Newman saw his team face Watford with much still to do. With the score at 0-0 the Rams were awarded a penalty but the lifeline was thrown away when Kevin Wilson fired the spot-kick straight at Steve Sherwood.

Now, though, Steve Sherwood looks aghast. Steve Buckley's spectacular shot has just put the Rams ahead. Eventually they won 3-2, the winning goal coming from Kevin Hector on his 589th and last appearance for the club.

Derby County began 1982-83 badly with a 3-0 home defeat by Carlisle United and a 4-1 defeat at QPR. There was only one League win in the first 16 games and after beating Chelsea at home in early September, the Rams did not taste victory again until December. On 11 September they drew 1-1 with Middlesbrough at the Baseball Ground. Andy Hill tries an overhead kick against 'Boro.

In November 1982 another Rams manager was sacked when John Newman lost his job. The Derby board turned to Brian Clough's former assistant, Peter Taylor, who was in retirement. One of Taylor's early matches in charge was right out of the story book – an FA Cup third-round tie against Clough's Nottingham Forest. The tie ensured that Cup fever returned to the Baseball Ground and on a dramatic afternoon, Derby won 2-0 with goals from Archie Gemmill and Andy Hill before a crowd of 28,494. Here Steve Sutton, making only his 13th senior appearance for Forest and later to join Derby, has no chance with Gemmill's spectacular goal from a free-kick.

Following riots on successive Saturdays at the Baseball Ground in January 1983, when visiting Leeds and Chelsea fans wrecked part of the Osmaston End of the ground, the Football Association held an inquiry at the ground. Here, FA chairman Sir Bert Millichip arrives to take part.

After beating Forest in the 1982-83 FA Cup, the Rams knocked out Chelsea, also at the Baseball Ground, before a visit from Manchester United in the fifth round. It was the last 30,000-plus attendance ever seen at the ground – 33,022 to be exact – and they saw United win 1-0 with a late goal from Norman Whiteside. Rams goalkeeper Steve Cherry gathers the ball watched by (from left to right) Steve Buckley, Archie Gemmill, Whiteside (10), Arnold Muhren, Steve Powell (hidden), Mick Brolly, George Foster, Remi Moses, John Barton and Frank Stapleton.

1982-83 was the season of Derby County's 'great escape'. By January they looked relegation certainties but only two defeats in their final 18 games saw them climb to 13th position by the end of the campaign. Even then, however, they could have gone down if results had been different on the final day of the season. The Rams entertained Fulham and won 1-0 with a Bobby Davison goal, but the game was soured by controversy when thousands of fans invaded the pitch and the referee ended the game 78 seconds early. Fulham, who might have been promoted had they won, wanted the match replayed – the Rams were safe anyway thanks to other results – but the FA refused. Here, Fulham goalkeeper Gerry Peyton can do nothing to stop Davison's shot.

Bobby Davison, arms raised, celebrates the goal that has ensured Derby's Second Division survival. John Barton rushes to congratulate him and referee Ray Chadwick signals the goal.

The result of yet another enquiry into the disgraceful scenes at the Fulham game was that the Rams had to play their first two home games of the 1983-84 season with the terraced areas of the Baseball Ground closed. This view from an empty Popular Side was taken during the 1-1 draw with Sheffield Wednesday on 29 August 1983. Two days earlier the Rams had opened the season with a 5-0 defeat at Stamford Bridge.

November 1983 was Derby County's best month of a dismal season. The Rams won two games and drew two more, including this 1-1 encounter with Leeds United in front of 16,974 spectators at the Baseball Ground. Derby goalkeeper Steve Cherry dives as Archie Gemmill and Eamonn Deacey police Leeds striker George McCluskey.

The FA Cup provided respite from an appalling League season in 1983-84. In the fourth round the Rams met non-League giantkillers Telford United in an intriguing tie at the Baseball Ground. There were no shocks, but it was a close thing as 21,000 saw Derby win 3-2 with a Bobby Davison hat-trick. The Telford goalkeeper collects the ball from the net while Davison goes on a little lap of honour while some Telford supporters were still making their way to the terraces.

The night of 14 March 1984 was a black one for Derby County. Amidst frequent High Court appearances in the struggle to save the club from extinction, and against a background of impending relegation, the Rams had reached the quarter-finals of the FA Cup after knocking out First Division Norwich City. In the sixth round Derby managed a goalless draw at Plymouth and went into the semi-final draw to be paired with Watford at Villa Park …if. It was a dream which didn't come true and Plymouth won the Cup replay 1-0 at the Baseball Ground after Steve Cherry blundered with a corner. Off the field, the news was also bleak: it appeared that the Rams were going out of business in their centenary year. Here Steve Powell, Calvin Plummer (on ground) and Bobby Davison cannot find a way through the Plymouth defence even with goalkeeper Crudgington also grounded.

There was no 'great escape' this time and in April 1984 Peter Taylor was sacked and Roy McFarland put in charge until the end of the season. McFarland did well but the task was too great. On 7 April, however, there was a little cheer when the Rams beat Crystal Palace 3-0 at the Baseball Ground and Andy Garner, a month past his 18th birthday, scored a hat-trick. He is the youngest player ever to hit three goals in one match for the Rams. Garner rounds Palace goalkeeper George Wood for one of his goals.

Bobby Davison watches as Garner hits another goal in his historic hat-trick against Crystal Palace. At the end of the season, though, Derby County were relegated to the Third Division for the first time in almost 30 years. The future of the club was safe, however, because director Stuart Webb had worked long and hard to bring Robert Maxwell's financial clout to bear in Derby's favour.

May 1984 and Stuart Webb introduces a new manager to Derby County. Arthur Cox, who once spent a lot of money on Chesterfield's behalf, has just walked out on Newcastle United despite having taken them to promotion from Division Two. We don't know it yet, but Cox will spend longer as manager of Derby County than anyone since George Jobey. He's also going to spend a lot of money.

10 October 1984: these are early days for Arthur Cox. Trailing 4-2 from the first leg of a League Cup second-round tie with Ipswich Town, the Rams managed a 1-1 draw against the First Division side at the Baseball Ground. Kevin Taylor is seen here appealing for a penalty as Bobby Davison is felled by Terry Butcher. Paul Hooks, Steve McCall and Russell Osman are the other players. The game attracted over 14,000 spectators.

Steve Sutton made his League debut for Derby County as long ago as 2 March 1985, when he was on loan from Nottingham Forest. He first appeared in a 1-1 draw against Rotherham United at the Baseball Ground. Here he is punching clear from Rotherham's Mike Pickering as Rob Hindmarch winces. The Rams ended their first season back in Division Three in seventh place.

16 November 1985: in the first round of the FA Cup for only the second time since 1956, the Rams beat Crewe Alexandra 5-1 at the Baseball Ground. Two-goal Trevor Christie goes up for a header with Alex's Steve Davis and Nick Longley.

Derby reached the fifth round of the FA Cup in 1986 before their run ended with 2-0 defeat in a second replay against Sheffield Wednesday at Hillsborough. In the first replay at the Baseball Ground, the pitch was bone hard on a freezing February evening and Wednesday goalkeeper Martin Hodge was knocked out after colliding with Bobby Davison. Hodge, who kept the Owls in the game with some fine saves to help them draw 1-1, is receiving attention.

1 October 1986: Derby County, now back in Division Two after finishing third the previous season, came from 2-0 behind to beat Sunderland 3-2 at the Baseball Ground with goals from Forsyth, Davison and Sage. Here Rams goalkeeper Mark Wallington flounders as a Sunderland forward nips in between Forsyth and Ross MacLaren.

2 May 1987: straight through from Third Division to First. Derby County won the Second Division title in 1986-87 and this victory over Leeds United at the Baseball Ground ensured promotion. Scoring sensation Phil Gee – 15 League goals in his first full season – leaves Brendan Ormsby trailing in his wake before cracking a low shot past Mervyn Day to give the Rams the lead.

Day hesitates following a Gary Micklewhite centre and Bobby Davison, who scored 19 League goals this season, nips in to send a glancing header into the Leeds net. 2-0 to Derby, who eventually won 2-1.

Leeds are beaten – none of the old animosity of the 1970s remains – and Derby are back in the top flight, so the carnival can begin. Nigel Callaghan applauds the crowd. Other players are (left to right) 'George' Williams, Eric Steele, John Gregory, Paul Blades and Mickey Forsyth.

Arthur Cox celebrates promotion to the First Division. His assistant Roy McFarland and Rams director Stuart Webb raise their glasses too. They all have chequered futures at the Baseball Ground. Cox will be around for quite a while yet, through ups and downs, financial windfalls, spending sprees and ultimate disappointment; McFarland will one day take over from Cox, but without the luxury of a seemingly bottomless pot of money to spend; Webb will be ousted from the board in yet another Baseball Ground power struggle. But he will return once more, under a new owner.

Arthur, you're our hero! Manager Arthur Cox went around the touch-line to shake hands with supporters. The fencing – mercifully dismantled in the wake of the Hillsborough tragedy – already looks old-fashioned. Did we really watch football in prison conditions?

26 June 1987: England goalkeeper Peter Shilton is pictured at the Baseball Ground having just joined the Rams from Southampton. One of new owner Robert Maxwell's national newspapers claims that it's a seven-figure signing. It isn't – no where near it in fact – but Shilton is still a great signing. A big name and still performing wonders between the posts. His Derby career will last for a few years and he will extend his remarkable appearances record still further in the Rams' colours.

10 October 1987: Shilton looks crestfallen now though, as do the inhabitants of the Pop Side. Paul Wilkinson of Nottingham Forest has just scored the only goal of the game at the Baseball Ground. Derby have won only two games so far this season, their first back in Division One under Arthur Cox.

16 March 1988: Liverpool came to the Baseball Ground still unbeaten in the First Division. They took the lead and then played around with the ball, passing it from man to man at the back. It annoyed Derby fans who were more than delighted when the Merseysiders paid the price for not pushing in search of extending their lead. Mickey Forsyth, not famed for his raiding qualities, stole in to score the equaliser. Phil Gee is mighty pleased as Bruce Grobbelaar is on his knees and the ball is in the back of the Liverpool net.

Former Arsenal and Manchester United striker Frank Stapleton, a Republic of Ireland international, scored only once in his brief career with Derby County, in this 2-0 win over Southampton at the Baseball Ground in April 1988. Here he hooks the ball past Kevin Moore as John Gregory and Phil Gee look on.

27 August 1988: the opening day of another season. Arthur Cox has signed an interesting player in Nigerian international winger John Chiedozie, from Spurs. Chiedozie, who used to play for Notts County, was an exciting player but had been dogged by injury. Alas, his Derby career was all too brief and he was soon side-lined again before being forced to call it a day. Here he takes the ball through a panicky Middlesbrough defence with goalkeeper Stephen Pears flat on his back. Trevor Hebberd is the Rams number ten. Derby won 1-0.

When Peter Shilton signed for the Rams he was soon joined by his former Southampton colleague, England international centre-half Mark Wright, who cost the Rams a club record £760,000. Wright proved a great success at Derby, albeit he ended up playing in a relegated team. His temper sometimes got the better of him, though. In the home game against Norwich City on 8 October 1988, Wright tangled with Canaries forward Trevor Putney (11). The Norwich player was already in trouble with the referee but Wright made quite a bit of ground to get involved. They were both sent off. It wasn't Wright's day – he had just scored the own-goal which settled the game.

Derby County broke their club transfer record again when they paid Oxford United £1 million for striker Dean Saunders, although some cynics might have said that Robert Maxwell, who owned both clubs, was simply moving his money – or someone else's – from one trouser pocket to another. It didn't matter to Rams fans, though. They loved 'Deano' from the moment he scored his first goal for the club. Here it is, a perfect header just steered past Wimbledon goalkeeper Hans Segers after Nigel Callaghan had crossed. The Rams beat the Dons 4-1 at the Baseball Ground in October 1988.

Paul Goddard watches as Wimbledon goalkeeper Hans Segers touches a Saunders shot on to the bar. It bounced down and into the net. Ted McMinn followed up to make sure but it was Saunders' goal, his second on his Rams debut.

11 November 1988: Dean Saunders' arrival coincided with Derby County's best position in years, finishing fifth in Division One in 1988-89. The next season they carried on the good work until injuries and the sale of Goddard interrupted matters. In this 6-0 rout of Manchester City the Rams were superb. Mark Wright opens the scoring after his header came back off Andy Dibble's crossbar and he lashes home the rebound. Left to right are Dibble, Hinchcliffe, Fleming, Wright, Goddard and Bracewell.

Against Manchester City, Ted McMinn tormented Gary Fleming all afternoon. Here the 'Tin Man' cracks in another shot as City do their best to weather the growing storm.

25 March 1989: Mickey Forsyth prepares to clear upfield as Nottingham Forest's Steve Hodge closes in at the Baseball Ground. Williams and Wright are in the background. Terry Wilson is number five for Forest, who won 2-0.

17 April 1989: after the Hillsborough tragedy, when 96 people were killed at the Forest-Liverpool FA Cup semi-final, fences came down at football grounds all over the country. A workman begins to dismantle the perimeter fencing which has for too long spoiled the view from the Baseball Ground terraces, necessary though the fences were when football hooliganism was at its most rife.

# The Nineties

The decade began with Derby still in Division One. But, as we later discovered, the Maxwell millions didn't exist. Lionel Pickering's did, though, but the massive spending spree got the Rams nowhere, despite two Play-offs. Rebuilding had to be the name of the game.

9 September 1989: Liverpool's Ian Rush gets a foot to the ball as Derby skipper Mark Wright tries to clear at the Baseball Ground. Derby lost 3-0.

25 October 1989: Dean Saunders tussles for the ball with Sheffield Wednesday's Nigel Worthington at the Baseball Ground. In this League Cup third round match the Rams trailed to a David Hirst penalty scored four minutes from time. But Saunders levelled the score from the spot and then hit the winner, all before the 90 minutes were up.

10 January 1990: Saunders is agonisingly close as he tries to beat Port Vale goalkeeper Mark Grew. Ray Walker is the other Vale player as the Rams tumble out of the FA Cup, 3-2 in a Baseball Ground replay. Grew was on loan to Derby in March 1986 but never made a senior appearance.

16 January 1990: Derby County's tallest player Kevin Francis, at 6ft 7in, towers over Geraint Williams, their smallest. Francis, the tallest footballer in the League, scored in the Port Vale replay but it was his only goal for the Rams. With his opportunities restricted at the Baseball Ground he moved to Stockport County, where he became a great favourite and a regular goalscorer. A move to Wimbledon broke down when he was injured but eventually Barry Fry paid £800,000 to take the big striker to Birmingham City. The Rams received one-third of that fee because of a sell-on clause when he moved to Edgeley Park.

12 March 1990: How did he do that? Future Derby County player Ian Ormondroyd dances away in delight after scoring the only goal of the game between Derby County and Aston Villa at the Baseball Ground. England colleagues Mark Wright and Peter Shilton look dumbfounded.

24 March 1990: another home defeat for the Rams, this time 3-1 to Arsenal. Gunners' two-goal hero Martin Hayes prods the ball past Peter Shilton, despite Mark Wright's challenge. Mickey Forsyth is at hand.

14 April 1990: When Derby beat Millwall at the Baseball Ground it ended a barren run of seven games. Mick Harford (right) celebrates one of his two goals with Mel Sage.

31 October 1990: Mick Harford celebrates again, this time over one of his hat-trick goals in the Rams' 6-0 League Cup win over Sunderland at the Baseball Ground. A rare treat in the dark, bitter days of the Maxwell stranglehold on the club.

During the 2-1 win over Nottingham Forest at the Baseball Ground on 24 November 1990, Mark Wright slides into the tackle on Nigel Jemson. Despite this famous victory, relegation was to follow at the end of a miserable, frustrating season.

21 September 1991: Derby's first season back in the Second Division took a boost when old favourite Bobby Davison returned on loan. Ian Ormondroyd also arrived and here against Brighton at the Baseball Ground he wins an aerial battle with Dean Wilkins. Mark Patterson is the other Rams player. Derby won 3-1.

5 October 1991: Loan signing Bobby Davison scored twice in this 4-1 thrashing of Bristol City – the first of four consecutive League wins for the Rams. Gary Micklewhite, who was also on the score-sheet, gets the better of City goalkeeper Keith Welch.

5 February 1992: what a splendid night this was, even if the Rams finally lost the FA Cup fourth-round tie to Aston Villa at the Baseball Ground. It was a seven-goal thriller, two Villa penalties and both saved by Shilton (although Yorke followed up to score from the rebound of one) and the Rams fighting back from 3-1 down. Phil Gee (9) has just scored for Derby. Ted McMinn is already on a lap of honour for his colleague.

Simon Coleman, who was bought to replace Mark Wright (who with Dean Saunders had been transferred to Liverpool in a multi-million pound move), tackles Dwight Yorke in the pulsating Cup-tie against Villa. Paul Williams and Ian Ormondroyd are the other Rams players.

Rams goalkeeper Peter Shilton holds a centre in front of his crossbar as Villa launch another attack. Comyn and Coleman are ready to help if required.

2 May 1992: After a brilliant run-in to the season the Rams were only minutes away from automatic promotion. Beating Swindon Town, they heard that promotion rivals Middlesbrough were trailing at Wolves. Even a draw at Molineux would have sent the Rams up but 'Boro scored two late goals. Here Paul Kitson has just given Derby the lead over Swindon and Andy Comyn and Mickey Forsyth celebrate with him.

13 May 1992: Derby County just missed automatic promotion after new owner Lionel Pickering's first massive injections of cash helped buy new players. It meant that they entered the Play-offs for a place in the new Premier League and when they were leading 2-0 in the first leg of the semi-final at Ewood Park, supporters were already making plans for Wembley. But Kenny Dalglish's Blackburn Rovers won 4-2 and in the second leg at the Baseball Ground Andy Comyn gave the Rams an early lead to rekindle their hopes. Tommy Johnson is so pleased that he hugs the scorer; Marco Gabbiadini is also in loving mood.

Alas, Derby's joy was short-lived. Blackburn are celebrating Kevin Moran's goal and, of course, it was Rovers who were eventually promoted and whose fortunes just went up and up. For Derby there was only the bitter taste of failure.

6 December 1992: Tommy Johnson places the ball past Swindon Town goalkeeper Nicky Hammond to give Derby the lead at the County Ground. The Rams won 4-2 to maintain a wonderful away record. It was a pity that their home form didn't match that of their travels.

Johnson wheels away to celebrate his 28th-minute goal at Swindon. During an ultimately disappointing campaign, this victory came in a club record of seven consecutive away victories.

8 March 1993: The Rams had a disappointing season in the League, never quite in the promotion race, but they did enjoy a run to the FA Cup quarter-finals. In the thrilling 3-3 home draw with Sheffield Wednesday, the Owls' Mark Bright tumbles from a challenge by Mark Patterson. A penalty resulted. Wednesday won the replay 1-0.

2 October 1993: on the day following the departure of manager Arthur Cox – he was suffering from a bad back – Roy McFarland took charge of the televised home game against West Brom and oversaw a 5-3 victory. Here Paul Kitson, who was later to be publicly critical of the new manager, controls the ball with Baggies' Darren Bradley in attendance.

New manager Roy McFarland discusses a point with chairman Brian Fearn while vice-chairman and owner Lionel Pickering, the man who bankrolled Arthur Cox's ultimately fruitless spending spree, looks thoughtful. Eventually Fearn would be ousted – there were many problems, not least the sale, against Pickering's wishes, of Paul Kitson to Newcastle for less than the owner valued him – and Pickering became chairman with his own board in place.

28 December 1993: Leicester City's Gary Coatsworth receives the red card after bringing down Tommy Johnson, who scored the winning goal as the Rams triumphed 3-2 in this festive encounter.

Johnson, recalled to the team for the game against Leicester, is mobbed by colleagues Gabbiadini, Harkes, Pembridge and Williams after scoring the winner against the Foxes.

15 May 1994: back in the Play-offs, looking for a place in the Premiership, the Rams scored a great victory in the semi-final against Millwall. The Lions' goalmouth is packed but Kasey Keller, the American goalkeeper, can do nothing to prevent Rams skipper Gordon Cowans (7) scoring his only goal for the club. Harkes is the other Derby player aloft wearing the number-four shirt.

Gordon Cowans is buried under his ecstatic colleagues. Tommy Johnson added a second and the Rams took a 2-0 lead to The New Den. Would it be enough?

In the hostile second leg of the 1994 First Division Play-off semi-final, the Rams scored a memorable 3-1 victory. Overall victory was in sight as early as the fourth minute when Marco Gabbiadini turned the ball past Keller, who is seen prostrate as Gabbiadini turns in joy. Sadly, violence from some Millwall fans soured the night but Derby were at Wembley.

With the First Division Play-off Final against Leicester City at Wembley only four days away, Craig Short shows off some of the special 'Wembley 94' merchandise. Alas, after Tommy Johnson had given the Rams a great start, Leicester scored a late goal in each half to gain promotion. They were a poor side, as their subsequent plight in the Premiership illustrated. We were left to wonder how Derby would have fared …if only.

22 January 1995: Paul Simpson hits his third goal to seal a 3-0 victory over Portsmouth at the Baseball Ground. New signing Paul Trollope is the other Derby player.

On 11 March 1995, Millwall visited the Baseball Ground and the Rams won 3-2 to maintain their excellent start to the month during which they eventually won five games on the trot and Roy McFarland received a Manager of the Month award. Here Marco Gabbiadini falls but makes it 3-1. Inset, Mark Pembridge opens the scoring with a fine first-half effort.

On 22 March there were more goals when Swindon Town were beaten 3-1 under the Baseball Ground floodlights. Here Paul Simpson cracks home an early penalty. Inset: Mark Pembridge was on target regularly after returning to the Rams side following his recovery from an injury which saw him miss a big chunk of the season. His goals were often spectacular, from long range, like this one which restored the Rams' lead against Swindon.

1 April but the Rams are no fools as Bristol City are beaten 3-1. This is the second goal, scored by Paul Williams (partly hidden), a powerful header through a crowded goalmouth. Right, top: Williams acknowledges the crowd after his goal. New signing Lee Mills, from Wolves, is about to offer his congratulations. Another relative newcomer, Paul Trollope, from Torquay United, is not far behind. Right, bottom: Youngster Darren Wrack scores his first senior goal for Derby County, against Bristol City to make it 3-1. Wrack had come on as substitute for Dean Yates, who Derby had signed from Notts County. The former Magpies centre-half impressed before he, too, fell victim to an injury which kept him out for the rest of the season.

Wednesday, 12 April. The Rams led fellow promotion challengers Wolves 3-1 after this goal by Paul Simpson. But in the dying seconds Wanderers levelled the scores to cost Derby two vital points. Their Play-off hopes were now almost over.

Far left: Paul Trollope has just scored at Turf Moor on Easter Saturday but the result was dreadful, the Rams going down 3-1 to soon-to-be-relegated Burnley.

Left: On Easter Monday, though, the Rams produced a five-goal performance against Tranmere Rovers, who also harboured hopes of a Play-off place. Mark Pembridge hammers home the first goal, his seventh of the season in the League.

Lee Mills is injured after scoring Derby's second goal against Tranmere, just before half-time.

Paul Williams adds to Tranmere's woe, heading home from a right-wing corner. Despite this marvellous victory, the Rams were clinging to only faint hopes which disappeared with a goalless draw at The Hawthorns five days later. Their great run had come too late for the club and for manager Roy McFarland whose departure was announced following a home defeat by Southend United. The decision, though, had apparently been taken 48 hours earlier. So, the manager was gone and several first-teamers also appeared to be on their way out of the Baseball Ground, itself soon to be redeveloped. Raymonds cameras will, of course, be there to record the ever changing story.